Catholic Update Guide to the Sacraments of Healing

Catholic Update
guide to the
Sacraments of Healing

Mary Carol Kendzia,
Series Editor

Cincinnati, Ohio

RESCRIPT
In accord with the *Code of Canon Law*, I hereby grant my *Imprimatur*
the *Catholic Update Guide to the Sacraments of Healing.*
Most Reverend Joseph R. Binzer
Vicar General and Auxiliary Bishop
of the Archdiocese of Cincinnati
Cincinnati, Ohio
May 30, 2012

The *Imprimatur* ("Permission to Publish") is a declaration that a book or pamphlet is considered to be free from doctrinal or moral error. It is not implied that those who have granted the *Imprimatur* agree with the contents, opinions or statements expressed.

Scripture passages have been taken from *New Revised Standard Version Bible,* copyright ©1989 by the Division of Christian Education of the National Council of the Churches of Christ in the U.S.A., and used by permission. All rights reserved.
Excerpts from the documents of Vatican II are adapted from the versions available at www.vatican.va.

Cover and book design by Mark Sullivan
Cover image © istockphoto | James Pauls

LIBRARY OF CONGRESS CATALOGING-IN-PUBLICATION DATA
Catholic update guide to the sacraments of healing / Mary Carol Kendzia, series editor.
p. cm.
ISBN 978-1-61636-431-1 (alk. paper)
1. Unction. 2. Extreme unction. 3. Sacraments—Catholic Church. 4. Healing—Religious aspects—Catholic Church. I. Kendzia, Mary Carol.
BX2292.C38 2012
234'.166—dc23

2012017999

ISBN 978-1-61636-431-1

Copyright ©2012, Franciscan Media. All rights reserved.
Published by Franciscan Media
28 W. Liberty St.
Cincinnati, OH 45202
www.FranciscanMedia.org

Printed in the United States of America.
Printed on acid-free paper.
12 13 14 15 16   5 4 3 2 1

Contents

About This Series vii

Introduction ix

Chapter One
    The Healing Sacrament of Reconciliation 1

Chapter Two
    The Healing Sacrament of the Anointing of the Sick 23

Conclusion 49

Sources 51

Contributors 52

About This Series

The Catholic Update guides take the best material from our bestselling newsletters and videos to bring you up-to-the-minute resources for your faith. Topically arranged for these books, the words you'll find in these pages are the same clear, concise, authoritative information you've come to expect from the nation's most trusted faith formation series. Plus, we've designed this series with a practical focus—giving the "what," "why," and "how to" for the people in the pews.

The series takes the topics most relevant to parish life— e.g., the Mass, sacraments, Scripture, the liturgical year—and draws them out in a fresh and straightforward way. The books can be read by individuals or used in a study group. They are an invaluable resource for sacramental preparation, RCIA participants, faith formation, and liturgical ministry training, and are a great tool for everyday Catholics who want to brush up on the basics.

The content for the series comes from noted authors such as Thomas Richstatter, O.F.M., Lawrence Mick, Leonard Foley, O.F.M., Carol Luebering, William H. Shannon, and others. Their theology and approach is grounded in Catholic practice and tradition, while mindful of current Church practice and teaching. We blend each author's style and approach into a voice that is clear, unified, and eminently readable.

Enrich your knowledge and practice of the Catholic faith with the helpful topics in the Catholic Update Guide series.

Mary Carol Kendzia
Series Editor

Introduction

The *Catechism of the Catholic Church* calls reconciliation and the anointing of the sick the "sacraments of healing." These sacraments continue Jesus's work of restoring health and bringing salvation.

In the *Catholic Update Guide to the Sacraments of Healing* we review the healing power of both sacraments and dispel some of the misconceptions about them. Note that the sacrament of reconciliation is also called confession, penance, conversion, and the sacrament of forgiveness. The sacrament of the anointing of the sick is often called extreme unction or the sacrament of the dying. The variety of names for these two sacraments suggests there is more than one way to understand them.

Forgiveness has always been a major part of the Christian message. John the Baptist provided a ritual for the forgiveness of sin (see Mark 1:4). Jesus echoed this theme in his preaching: "I did not come to call the righteous but sinners" (see Mark 2:17).

The Church preached forgiveness and exercised Jesus's authority to forgive sins in a variety of ways. "Whose sins you forgive are forgiven them" (see John 20:23).

Jesus linked physical healing with forgiveness of sins on several occasions. His immediate response to a paralytic was, "Your sins are forgiven." When bystanders questioned whether a man could forgive sins, Jesus replied, "Which is easier? To say, 'Your sins are forgiven' or to say 'Rise and walk?'" And to show that he had authority he cured the paralyzed man (see Mark 2:1–12).

While both sacraments of healing are firmly rooted in Sacred Scripture, their application shows several stages of development. History records that formal reconciliation was reserved for notorious sinners and included excommunication from public worship until certain penances were performed. Sometime in the seventh century the process of reconciliation was extended to all Christians, even to those with minor sins.

All Christians could administer anointing of the sick with oil. Pope Innocent I wrote to a fifth-century bishop that the holy oil consecrated by the bishop "may be used not only by sacred ministers but by all Christians for anointing in the case of their own or other people's sickness."

With the passage of time and the tightening of controls, reconciliation became an obligation for all Catholics (Fourth Lateran Council, 1215) and anointing of the sick could be administered only by priests and bishops (Council of Trent, 1545–1563). The teaching of the Council of Trent challenged reformers who denied that this anointing was truly a sacrament instituted by Christ, and that the faithful who scorned the sacrament in the approach of death were guilty of sin.

The sacrament of reconciliation and the sacrament of the anointing of the sick are two of the ways that the Church formally continues Jesus's healing mission. In this *Catholic Update Guide to the Sacraments of Healing* we will review the what, why, and how of these two sacraments.

CHAPTER ONE

The Healing Sacrament of Reconciliation

What Is Reconciliation?

Father Thomas Richstatter, O.F.M., explains what we mean by the sacrament of reconciliation. He begins with a story that happened in the 1930s when Fr. Bernard Häring, a moral theologian, was the pastor of a parish in Germany. During a weekly class Fr. Häring was talking about confession, and began by asking the congregation, "What is the most important thing about confession?" A woman in the front pew immediately answered, "Telling your sins to the priest. That's why we call it *confession*." Fr. Häring said, "Confessing your sins is important, but it's not the most important thing."

A man toward the back called out, "Contrition! Being sorry for your sins! The whole thing doesn't work without contrition." Fr. Häring said, "That's right, it doesn't 'work' without contrition, but I don't think that contrition is the *most* important thing."

A man over on the left side of church spoke up. "It's the examination of conscience. Unless you examine your conscience, you don't know what you have to be sorry for and you don't know what to confess. Anybody can see that the examination of conscience is the most important thing." Fr. Häring wasn't satisfied with this answer either.

A young woman on the aisle tried: "It's the penance—giving back the things you stole—unless you do penance, it doesn't count." The congregation could tell by Fr. Häring's face that he still hadn't heard the most important thing. An uneasy silence fell over the church as the people tried to think.

In the silence a little girl in the third pew said, "Father, I know what's most important. It's what Jesus does!" Fr. Häring smiled. She had it right. It's what Jesus does!

Fr. Richstatter explains some of the history and theology of the sacrament in the following section.

* * *

As most of us know, our ritual has been growing through the centuries. I became aware of this back in the 1970s, while I was a student of Fr. Pierre Jounel, one of the principal authors of the revised *Rite of Penance*, a revision mandated by the Second Vatican Council. I learned that we have moved from a time when baptism and Eucharist were the *only* sacramental form of reconciliation to (1) canonical penance, whose paradigm (model) is baptism, to (2) Celtic penance, whose paradigm is a doctor visit, to (3) confession, whose paradigm is a legal trial. Now, in the light of Vatican II, we are in transition to (4) the sacrament of reconciliation, whose paradigm is Eucharist.

What Was Canonical Penance?

All sins are forgiven when we plunge into the death and resurrection of Jesus at baptism. In the early Church, sins committed after baptism were forgiven by prayer, almsgiving, fasting, self-denial, and especially by the Eucharist. But there were times when baptized Christians committed such grave, public, and scandalous sins that the community felt it was impossible to share the Eucharist with them.

The Church, empowered by the Holy Spirit to continue the reconciling ministry of Jesus, developed sacramental rites to help these sinners repent, convert, and be readmitted to the Eucharist. These rituals, which we now call "canonical penance," were modeled on the rituals for baptism and the catechumenate (the process for being admitted to baptism). They were public, liturgical, and—like baptism—they could be celebrated only once in a lifetime.

What Was Celtic Penance?

In fifth-century Ireland, we find a different type of penance. Celtic monks were accustomed to seek out a holy person to ask for advice in overcoming their sins—just as today we might go to a doctor to ask for help and advice in overcoming a physical illness.

The Christians would go to a holy monk, tell their sins, and ask for healing. Celtic penance was for all sins, not just grave, public sins. And, unlike canonical penance, the process was repeatable. The emphasis is not on "telling the sin" but on performing the penance; just as when we go to the doctor the main thing is not "confessing" our illness but doing what the doctor says and taking the medicine so that the illness will be healed.

What Was the Confession Model?

During the seventh century, Irish missionaries brought Celtic penance to Europe, and it eventually became "confession." In this expression of the sacrament, confession was to a priest who had the power to give absolution. The penance the sinner was to perform was greatly reduced: "fast on bread and water for ten years" became, for example, "say six Our Fathers." The emphasis is on the telling of sins to the priest (confession) and the priest's words of absolution.

When I made my first confession I knew that it was one of the seven sacraments, but my experience of confession was more a "devotional" experience than a "liturgical" experience. Liturgical elements—vestments, candles, music—were minimal or nonexistent.

At a time when the liturgy was in Latin and only devotional prayers were in the vernacular, in confession the priest and the penitent spoke to each other in the vernacular. Only the "formula of absolution" was in Latin (but usually I never heard it because the priest said it at the same time I was saying my Act of Contrition).

The pope of my youth, Pius XII, in his encyclical letter *Mediator Dei: On The Sacred Liturgy* (1947) writes about confession in the part of the encyclical entitled "Other Devotions Not Strictly Liturgical, Warmly Recommended." Apparently, even the pope thought of confession as devotional prayer!

Like other devotional prayers—the rosary, the Way of the Cross—confession, for some Catholics, has continued relatively unaffected by the liturgical reforms of the Second Vatican Council. But many Catholics stopped going to confession during the years following the Council. During the first half of the twentieth century, Catholics went to confession more frequently than they went to Holy Communion! But then—rather abruptly—around 1965, the long lines for confession on Saturday afternoons disappeared.

Various explanations are given. Some point to the encyclical *Humanae Vitae* (1968), with its unpopular ban on birth control.

Bishops speak of "the loss of the sense of sin." Some laity report that they have found other ways to experience what they used to receive from confession: support groups, Bible study, Alcoholics Anonymous, and so on. Some point out that the lines for confession became shorter as the lines for Holy Communion became longer. Many Catholics began to see Eucharist as the primary sacrament of reconciliation.

Vatican II's Revision

The Second Vatican Council (1962–1965) looked at the history of the ways in which the Church has exercised the power to forgive sins and, considering the cultural needs of the time, asked that the rituals for the sacrament of penance be revised "so that they more clearly express both the nature and the effects of the sacrament" (*Constitution on the Liturgy,* 72). The revised Rite of Penance was approved by Pope Paul VI in 1973 and was introduced in the United States on the First Sunday of Lent in 1976.

In my pastoral experience as I travel around the country giving workshops and parish missions, I find that the new ritual has not been widely implemented. It was the last of the sacraments to be revised; perhaps after ten years of liturgical change, we were worn out by so many modifications in the Mass, adult baptism, etc. Maybe we simply had renewal fatigue.

I find four categories of expression of the sacrament in parishes today: (1) devotional confession; (2) confession with spiritual direction; (3) communal Bible service followed by individual confession; and (4) communal penance services using the revised ritual. (I know these four categories are an oversimplification and that you will find many variations within each of these categories.)

Devotional Confession

I find that many people continue to go to confession just as they did before the new ritual. They come in, kneel down, repeat the traditional formula, recite a list of sins, and then wait for the priest to give a penance. They say an Act of Contrition and I give absolution. Like most devotions, part of the appeal of this ritual is its familiarity. And the penitent goes away with that good feeling that we receive from the performance of our devotions.

Spiritual Direction

Growth in the spiritual life is the motive for many Catholics to seek spiritual direction. For some Catholics, confession is their only opportunity to speak with a priest. In this expression of the sacrament, the person tells the state of their soul, their sins, and their temptations. I listen and give a word of encouragement. Personally I try not to give any advice. I simply do not have enough information. Spiritual direction and the sacrament of reconciliation are two distinct practices, and each works best in its own context. Spiritual direction is most effective through an established relationship between the person seeking direction and the director (who may or may not be a priest).

Bible Service Followed by Individual Confession

In some parishes, especially during Advent and Lent, there will be a Bible service consisting of a reading from Scripture, a homily, an examination of conscience, and an Act of Contrition. After these elements are completed several priests are available to hear individual confessions.

Communal Celebration

The revised ritual has a section called "Rite for Reconciliation of Several Penitents with Individual Confession and Absolution." While this ritual may look similar to the "Bible service" version, it is radically different. The most important change is not in the external ritual; it is much deeper. My first insight into this profound difference came from the story about Fr. Häring and the girl who said that the most important thing about confession is what Jesus does. Indeed the focus of the sacrament of reconciliation *is* on what God does for us.

Sacraments are acts of worship in which we gather to celebrate what God has done for us. In reconciliation we do not celebrate our sinfulness. We celebrate *who God is* and what God has done for us in Christ. This is very different from my memories of the dark confessional, of fearing the priest, of telling all my sins, of worrying whether I forgot something big. In that setting I was focused on what I was doing (confessing) rather than on what God was doing (forgiving). However you celebrate the sacrament, remember the most important thing: "what Jesus does!" Amen!

Why Do We Need Reconciliation?

Even if you understand the need to be forgiven, you may still be asking yourself, "Why should I go to confession? Won't God forgive me even if I don't receive the sacrament of reconciliation?"

Sister Sandra DeGidio, O.S.M., addresses this very question. She explains that Church law requires that we confess serious sins (see *CCC*, 1448, 1491), but that we also have a human need to confess and experience God's forgiveness.

* * *

Human beings do not live in their minds alone. We need to externalize bodily—with words, signs, and gestures—what is in our minds and hearts. We need to see, hear, and feel forgiveness—not just think about it.

We need other human beings to help us externalize what is within and open our hearts before the Lord, which puts the priest-confessors in a new light. They are best seen, not as faceless and impersonal judges, but as guides in our discernment, compassionately helping us experience and proclaim the mercy of God in our lives. As the Introduction to the Rite of Penance puts it, the confessor "fulfills a parental function...reveals the heart of the Father and shows the image of the Good Shepherd."

Another of the confessor's roles is to say the prayer of absolution. Contrary to what we may have thought in the past, this prayer, which completes or seals the penitent's change of heart, is not a prayer asking for forgiveness. It is a prayer signifying God's forgiveness of us and our reconciliation with the Church—which is certainly something to celebrate.

Externalizing What Is Within

Although we often call this sacrament "confession," in truth confessing sins is not the most important part. Confession of sin can be sincere only if the process of conversion precedes it. Confession is simply the externalizing of the interior transformation. This does not mean that confession of sin is unimportant, but it does mean that we need to go to confession to give external expression to the interior conversion.

Consider the parable of the prodigal son. The father, seeing his son in the distance, runs out to meet him with an embrace and a kiss. Through one loving gesture, the father forgives his son—and the son hasn't even made his confession yet! When he does confess, the father hardly listens. The confession then is not the most important thing here; the important thing is that the son got up and returned home.

Formerly the Rite of Reconciliation began with the penitent's saying, "Bless me, Father, for I have sinned." The revised rite directs the priest to welcome the penitent warmly and greet him with kindness. The priest is to offer a prayer, such as "May God, who has enlightened every heart, help you to know your sins and trust in his mercy." It is the confessor who takes the initiative, reaching out, welcoming the penitent, and creating a hospitable environment of acceptance and love before there is any naming of sins. Thus, this sacramental moment of confession—just one of the sacramental moments in the whole rite—focuses on God's love rather than on our sins.

It's a Celebration

Asking, "Why go to confession?" is similar to asking, "Why throw a party?" Parties are for celebrating. There is an inclination in the human psyche to express in an external way something of value or some cause for joy. Birthdays, weddings, anniversaries, promotions, and even reconciliations are reasons to celebrate. Grandma's ninetieth birthday or the reunion of estranged family members usually prompts a dinner or party. The happiness and joy of such occasions spill over into external forms we call celebrations.

The Hebrew word *halal* means "to shine," but in some contexts it can be translated "to praise, to boast, to celebrate." A married couple that celebrates a golden wedding anniversary is in fact boasting. The sacred liturgy of the Catholic Church is normally described as a celebration, an act of praise. Confession or reconciliation is a reason to celebrate, to give God praise, to boast.

One of the basic reasons for going to confession is therefore intimately tied to the normal expressions of human nature. When we have reason to be glad we celebrate, and the sacrament of reconciliation is in the Church's liturgy the "public" way of celebrating God's forgiveness of our sins.

Admittedly celebration is not a word most people associate with the sacrament of reconciliation. But in Jesus's parable of the prodigal son, celebration is obviously important and imperative. The father says to his servants, "Quickly bring the finest robe and put it on him; put a ring on his finger and sandals on his feet. Take the fattened calf and slaughter it. Then let us celebrate with a feast, because this son of mine was dead, and has come to life again; he was lost and has been found." And the celebration began (see Luke 15:22–24).

Celebration makes sense only when there is really something to celebrate. Each of us has had the experience of going to gatherings with all the trappings of a celebration—people, food, drink, balloons, bands—and yet the festivity was a flop for us. For example, attending an office party can be such an empty gathering for the spouse or friend of an employee. Celebration flows from lived experience or it is meaningless. The need for celebration to follow common lived experiences is especially true of sacramental celebrations. All of the sacraments are communal celebrations of the lived experience of believing Christians.

Penance as Conversion From Rugged Individualism

Perhaps what we need to help us feel more comfortable with the idea of celebration in relation to reconciliation is a conversion from our own rugged individualism. Let's face it—there is something about believing in a bogeyman God from whom we have to earn forgiveness that makes us feel good psychologically. It's harder to feel good about a God who loves and forgives us unconditionally—whether we know it or not, whether we want it or not, whether we like it or not. In the face of such love and forgiveness we feel uncomfortable. It creates a pressure within us that makes us feel as though we should "do something" to deserve such largess—or at least feel a little bit guilty.

The older brother in the parable of the prodigal son expresses this discomfort. Upon witnessing the festivities, he appeals to fairness and legalism. In sense, he is hanging on to the courtroom image of the sacrament of reconciliation, suggesting that there is no way everyone can feel good about the return of the younger brother until amends have been made.

But this older son is far too narrow in his understanding of life, of God, and of the sacrament. He is too calculating, too quantitative. This son finds it difficult to understand that we are never *not* forgiven. The sacrament of reconciliation does not bring about something that was absent. It proclaims and enables us to own God's love and forgiveness that are already present.

The older brother's problem is a universal human one. It's tough for most of us to say, "I'm sorry." It is even tougher to say, "You're forgiven." And it is most difficult of all to say gracefully, "I accept your forgiveness." To be able to do that we must be able to forgive ourselves. That, too, is one of the reasons we need to receive the sacrament.

The community's liturgical celebration of reconciliation places a frame around the picture of our continual journey from sin to reconciliation. Only someone who has never experienced or reflected on that journey will fail to understand the need for celebrating a sacrament.

The older son in Jesus's parable is likely such a person. When the father calls for a celebration, everyone else in the household responds. Not only do they celebrate the younger son's return, they celebrate their own experience of forgiveness, mercy, and reconciliation as well. They, like us, have been on that journey from which the young man has returned.

So there is something we can do about the unconditional forgiveness we receive from God—we can celebrate! And further we can forgive as we have been forgiven. Having been forgiven we are empowered to forgive ourselves and to forgive one another. We are celebrating that we have experienced the peace, justice, and reconciliation that makes us heralds of Christ's kingdom on earth.

A Communal Celebration

Since the revised rites for the sacrament of reconciliation provide opportunities for communal celebrations, we find still another reason why we should go to confession.

Theologians say that sacramental theology is not just vertical (between us and God) but it is also horizontal (between ourselves and others). Sacraments happen in people who are in relationship with each other as well as with God. In the area of sin and forgiveness and reconciliation, this horizontal relationship is obvious. Our sinfulness disrupts our relationship in the community as well as our relationship with God.

Since the sacrament of reconciliation includes conversion not only to God but to our brothers and sisters as well, it is only proper that it culminate with a communal expression of love and forgiveness that embodies the love and forgiveness of God. In the rite for reconciliation of several penitents with individual confession and absolution, the sacrament shows clearly this communal dimension. The instruction for the ritual explains, "The faithful listen together to the word of God, which as it proclaims his mercy invites them to conversion; at the same time they examine the conformity of their lives with that word of God and help each other through common prayer."

Unconverted "older sons" will always be out of step with the Christian community. When we celebrate the sacrament, we celebrate with joy and thanksgiving because the forgiveness of the

Christian community and of God has brought us to this moment—and that is worth celebrating. There is no room for the attitude that forgiveness comes only when you have recited your sins and agreed to suffer for them and thereby earn God's forgiveness. The celebration of the sacrament, especially in its communal form, underscores that we are all sinners, but God loves us anyway.

The "older sons" among us are looking for what theologian Dietrich Bonhoeffer called "cheap grace," that is, grace without discipleship, without the cross, without faith, without humility, without Jesus Christ. The "younger sons" among us, however, have more than ample reason to come to the Lord in the sacrament of reconciliation and allow the Father to put his arms around us and hold us close to his loving and forgiving heart.

Church Law and the Need for the Sacrament

Not everyone is persuaded that we need to receive the sacrament of reconciliation in order to externalize our conversion and to celebrate God's unconditional love. For this reason the Church gives added weight to its theology by enacting laws about receiving the sacrament. Church laws 988 and 989 oblige the Christian faithful to confess "in kind and number all grave sins committed after baptism," and further stipulates that "each member of the faithful is obliged to confess faithfully his or her grave sins at least once a year."

The Rite of Penance itself urges "frequent and careful celebration of this sacrament" as a useful remedy for venial sins. It explains, "This is not a mere ritual repetition or psychological exercise, but a serious striving to perfect the grace of baptism so that, as we bear in our body the death of Christ, his life may be seen in us ever more clearly" (see 2 Corinthians 4:10).

The *Catechism of the Catholic Church* (1426–1428) describes the sacrament of reconciliation as a second conversion, which it describes as "an uninterrupted task for the whole Church." Baptism is the principal expression for the first and fundamental conversion, but Christian initiation does not abolish the weakness of human nature. The struggle of conversion is lifelong. We need the sacrament of reconciliation because we are still on the way to responding to Christ's call.

How We Receive the Sacrament of Reconciliation

For the penitent (the one confessing) there are four parts to the Rite of Penance:

1. contrition (sorrow for sin);
2. confession (acknowledging the sins to the priest);
3. act of penance (an act or prayer which the confessor imposes on the penitent);
4. absolution (the priest-confessor assures the penitent of God's forgiveness).

Before going to confession, the penitent normally will spend some time in what is popularly called an "examination of conscience." Unfortunately, many penitents think this examination is simply reviewing the Ten Commandments to see which ones they have broken, but it is more than going over a list of sins.

A true examination of conscience includes recalling one's relationship with God (recalling God's goodness, love, and mercy) and asking, "How have I responded to this relationship? Have I lived up to my baptismal promises?" It is in the light of this examination that a penitent formulates the sins he or she will confess.

Church law (canon 960) says that individual and integral confession and absolution constitute the only ordinary means by which a member of the faithful who is conscious of grave sin is reconciled with God and the Church. Canon 988 says one is obliged to confess "in kind and in number" all grave sins committed after baptism and not yet remitted directly through the keys of the Church. This canon also recommends confession of venial sins.

The Vatican II revision of how the sacrament of reconciliation can be celebrated allows for three ritual forms:

1. Rite for reconciliation of individual penitents;
2. Rite for reconciliation of several penitents with individual confession and absolution;

3. Rite for reconciliation of penitents with general confession and absolution.

The first rite usually takes place in a confessional or reconciliation room; only the penitent and priest-confessor are present. The second rite usually occurs with a gathering of several penitents in a penance service (i.e., song, prayer, Scripture, homily, examination of conscience, an act of contrition, and the Lord's Prayer) followed by individual confession. Rite three is seldom used since absolution without prior, individual confession cannot be given collectively except when there is danger of death or there are not enough confessors present to accommodate the crowd.

A Closer Look at the Communal Celebration

Fr. Thomas Richstatter, O.F.M., offers additional insights about the second ritual, the communal celebration (several penitents with individual confession). He notes that many Catholics have moved from individual confession to communal celebrations. In parishes across the United States we can find large numbers of Catholics participating in the communal sacrament of reconciliation, especially before Easter and Christmas. His explanation continues in the passage below.

* * *

Communal celebrations show more clearly that reconciliation is a sacrament, a corporate act of worship. When we celebrate together as a parish family, we are reminded of the social nature of sin—that every sin, even the most private and personal sin, has implications for the larger community. In addition, we are reminded of our obligation to "forgive those who trespass against us" even as we ask God to forgive us our trespasses.

The communal ritual receives its shape from the ritual for the Eucharist. Think of a typical Thanksgiving meal. There are four movements:

1. we come together;
2. we tell our stories and talk about what happened since last we met;
3. we move to the table and eat;
4. we take our leave and go our separate ways.

The revised rite for the sacrament of reconciliation has this same fourfold structure:

1. we gather as a community to form the Body of Christ;
2. we recall our sacred story (Scripture), which urges our ongoing conversion;
3. we celebrate God's forgiveness in reconciliation;
4. we return to the world resolved to live the Gospel and sin no more.

The most important thing in the sacrament of reconciliation, you will remember, is what Jesus does. While the examination of conscience, sorrow for sin, telling the sins to the priest, and acts of satisfaction (the penance we receive) are all important elements on our part, the key to understanding what we do is to make us aware of what Jesus does: he welcomes us, assures us of forgiveness, and encourages us to continue living the values of the Gospel.

Questions for Reflection
1. How does reconciliation help heal our relationships with God and others?
2. How does "externalizing the interior" help us appreciate reconciliation?
3. Why do we use the term "celebration" about reconciliation?

CHAPTER TWO

The Healing Sacrament of the Anointing of the Sick

We sometimes hear Jesus called "the divine physician." Even a passing familiarity with the Gospels reveals that Jesus was constantly healing the sick and assuring people, "Your sins are forgiven." The apostles and consequently the Church were instructed by Jesus to carry on this ministry. "Heal the sick," he said (see Matthew 10:8).

The early Church formulated a ritual in response to Jesus's command. We find it recorded in the Letter of James: "Are any among you sick? They should call for the elders of the church and have them pray over them, anointing them with oil in the name of the Lord. This prayer of faith will save the sick, and the Lord will raise them up; and anyone who has committed sins will be forgiven" (5:14–15).

Fr. Richstatter explores the nature of the sacrament of the anointing of the sick. His thoughts begin as he recalls how surprised he was when he saw how many passages tell of Jesus's healing ministry.

* * *

At the beginning of Mark's Gospel, Jesus calls the first disciples, cures a man with an unclean spirit, and then cures Peter's mother-in-law, who is in bed with a fever. That same evening, "they brought him all who were sick or possessed with demons. And the whole city was gathered around the door" (Mark 1:32–33). All this in only the first chapter!

Jesus gives us a sign, a sacrament of God's desire for our health and wholeness. Jesus is the original sacrament of healing. Jesus "spoke to them about the kingdom of God, and healed those who needed to be healed" (Luke 9:11b). Jesus commissioned the Twelve to continue his ministry in word and work. "So they went out and proclaimed that all should repent. They cast out many demons, and anointed with oil many who were sick and cured them" (Mark 6:12–13).

The healing ministry of Jesus is to be continued by the Church, as we see from the ending of Mark's Gospel. There the Risen Christ tells the Eleven, "Go into all the world and proclaim the good news to the whole creation.... And these signs will accompany those who believe: …they will lay their hands on the sick, and they will recover" (Mark 16:15b, 17a, 18b).

The Second Vatican Council restored the sacrament of the anointing of the sick to the context of prayer and mutual concern that we find in the Epistle of James. The anointing of the sick had suffered many distortions with the passage of time. It had been given the name "extreme unction" (the "last anointing" or "anointing *in extremis*") and had been turned into a sacrament of the dying. It was feared by many and usually postponed until the last moments of life. This was a situation that needed to be corrected.

And more has changed than the sacrament's name. Our experience of the revised sacrament of anointing has brought about a change in the ways we think about the sacrament. For example: (1) This sacrament (like all sacraments) is a community celebration; (2) sickness involves more than just bodily illness; and (3) anointing heals us through faith.

The practice of administering extreme unction to those who were at the point of death brought with it a certain privatization of the sacrament. While we have become accustomed to the sacrament's new name, many Catholics still think of it as a private sacrament, administered by a priest to a single individual.

If I asked you to close your eyes and picture the sacrament of anointing, what image would come to your mind? I think many Catholics would picture a priest standing at a hospital bedside.

For an increasing number of Catholics, however, the mental picture would be different. They would picture a parish gathered for Sunday Eucharist, with thirty or so people—some visibly ill, some apparently perfectly healthy—coming up the aisle to be anointed, some with their spouses or caregivers.

That public, communal sacrament is the sacrament celebrated to its fullest. One of the general principles of the Second Vatican Council's renewal of Catholic worship states: "Liturgical services are not private functions, but are celebrations belonging to the Church.... Therefore liturgical services involve the whole Body of the Church; they manifest it and have effects upon it.... Whenever rites...make provision for communal celebration involving the presence and active participation of the faithful, it is to be stressed that this way of celebrating is to be preferred, as far as possible, to a celebration that is individual and, so to speak, private" (*Constitution on the Sacred Liturgy*, 26–27).

We are gradually experiencing this change among other sacraments too. I can remember priests often saying their private Mass at the church's side altars; today side altars have disappeared from our churches as we come to see Eucharist as a community celebration. The baptism of adult converts at the Easter Vigil has become public in a way and to an extent I would never have imagined before the Second Vatican Council.

We are coming to see the sacrament of the anointing of the sick in a similar fashion. In Vatican II's *Constitution on the Church,* we find this theology: "By the sacred anointing of the sick and the prayer of the priests the *whole Church* commends those who are ill to the suffering and glorified Lord that he may raise them up and save them…" (11, emphasis added).

The *Catechism of the Catholic Church* states that when the sick are anointed they should be "assisted by their pastor and the whole ecclesial community, which is invited to surround the sick in a special way through their prayers and fraternal attention" (*CCC*, 1516). "Like all the sacraments the anointing of the sick is a liturgical and communal celebration…. It is very fitting to celebrate it within the Eucharist" (*CCC*, 1517).

More and more parishes today are scheduling celebrations of the sacrament of the anointing of the sick within the Eucharist. Pastors have told me that these communal celebrations educate the parish about the meaning of the sacrament and help to break down some of the fear that still remains from the days of extreme unction. These celebrations speak eloquently about the key themes of Christian life: mortality, vocation, responsibility, limits, suffering, caregiving. Communal celebration of healing and trusting in God speaks loudly to a society that stresses individual responsibilities and tends to avoid discussing limits and mortality.

The Meaning of Sacraments

To better understand the "what" of the anointing of the sick it is helpful to review briefly the whole notion of "sacrament." Sr.

Sandra DeGidio, O.S.M., thinks of the seven sacraments as "symbols of God's care." She writes that sacraments are, as St. Augustine said, "visible expressions of invisible grace." They effect what they signify. They can and do effect a change in us if we are ready to accept that change. The marvelous mystery of God's grace is that, while it is always there awaiting our recognition and acceptance of it in our lives, in that very recognition and celebration the gift becomes even more present to us. Her explanation continues below.

* * *

The grace of the sacraments can only be spoken of in *relational* terms. The new rites for the sacraments repeatedly speak of a deeper relationship or greater conformity with Christ and the Church. Sacraments do not happen simply to individuals, but to Christ's body, the Church. And when something happens to the Church, it happens to the individual as well. For this reason the new rites insist that the sacraments be celebrated in the Christian assembly, with the community present and actively participating. The symbols in the sacraments are communal; the richness and effectiveness of the symbolism often depends on our degree of participation and responsiveness. The grace of the sacraments is the grace of the Church in service to others.

In the light of DeGidio's explanation of sacraments in general, we can see that the sacrament of the anointing of the sick brings the individual and the community together in a grace-filled encounter with God. The sick person gives witness to the suffering and fragility that mark human life. The sick who receive the anointing allow their infirmity, in a very concrete way, to waken within the Church an awareness of both our brokenness and our need to support one another. Their illness, publicly acknowledged, invites prayer, promotes compassion, and shares in the efficacy of the sufferings of Jesus Christ.

The sacrament of the anointing of the sick, as the general introduction to the revised rite explains, gives the grace of the Holy Spirit to those who are ill and strengthens them against the temptations of the devil and against anxiety about dying. Through this sacrament the sick person is empowered to bear the suffering bravely and even fight against it. And "the sacrament also provides the sick person with the forgiveness of sins and the completion of Christian penance" (*Pastoral Care of the Sick*, 6).

Jesus Cures, the Church Heals

The New Testament confirms Jesus's concern for the sick and broken members of society. People flocked to him to be cured. Mark writes that one evening the ill and the possessed were brought to Jesus, that he cured many who were sick with a variety of diseases, and that "the whole city was gathered around the door" (see Mark 1:33). Matthew records Jesus's commissioning his disciples to go out and preach the kingdom and to "cure the sick, raise the dead, cleanse the lepers, cast out demons" (see Matthew 10:8). In his First Letter to the Corinthians, Paul writes about the many spiritual gifts that the Spirit gives, including the gifts of healing (12:9, 28, 30).

The Church from the beginning recognized Jesus's healing ministry and believed it was part of its mission to continue his practice. Luke recalls in the Acts of the Apostles that people brought the sick out into the streets so that when Peter passed by his "shadow might fall on some of them" and they might be cured (see 5:15). And James writes in his letter that the sick are to be anointed with oil in the name of the Lord that they may be saved, that the Lord may raise them up, and their sins may be forgiven (see 5:13–15).

It is this last reference (James 5:13–15) that serves as the biblical basis for the Church's practice of anointing the sick and insisting that this anointing is worthy to be called a sacrament. The Gospel of Mark records that the apostles were sent out to preach, to exorcise, and to heal. The evangelist specifically notes that they "anointed with oil many who were sick and cured them" (6:13).

Jesus's concern and the Church's practice respond to the threat posed by physical sickness, spiritual illness, and human mortality. To put it simply, disease, disfigurement, depression, and death cause pain and fear. Trauma, whether physical or mental, is a human response to the presence (or threat) of serious injury. We do not have a diagnosis of the fever which disabled Peter's mother-in-law, but we do know that Jesus was compassionate and healed her (see Mark 1:30–31).

Even though pain and suffering play an essential role in human development and have a special place in Jesus's plan for salvation, the Lord seldom hesitated to apply the healing touch and restore health. Catholics receive the sacrament of the anointing of the sick that they may experience that healing touch. Even when a cure does not result from the anointing, a certain healing will.

The Effects of the Sacrament

What does the sacrament of anointing do for the person who receives it? James 5:15 claims three effects: "The prayer of faith will save the sick, and the Lord will raise them up; and anyone who has committed sins will be forgiven." For a person who is sick or dying, reception of these three effects is a consummation devoutly to be wished: to be saved, to be raised up, to be forgiven.

The problem, however, is that these three effects do not always show up. Experience shows that most people who receive the sacrament are not physically cured by it. If the Church is continuing Jesus's ministry, should we not have cures by the dozens every day? The difficulty for us, then, is to determine what the saving, the raising up, and the forgiving really mean. And here we are face-to-face with the mystery of God's will and our speculation about it.

Some well-meaning people say that a sick person who is not cured must lack faith. After all, James did say, "the prayer of faith will save the sick" (see James 5:15). And he goes on to assert that "the prayer of the righteous is powerful and effective" (see James 5:16). And further still, James cites Elijah as an example of a human being who prayed and heaven responded. Consequently, if the minister of the sacrament had more faith, if the sick or dying person had more faith, then a cure would take place—or so these well-meaning souls try to explain.

Accusing the sick or dying of a lack of faith hardly seems compassionate at a time when compassion is called for. It is hard to believe that all those whom Jesus cured had huge quantities of faith. Although lack of faith by the people was a problem for Jesus, it obviously did not stop his exorcising demons, raising the dead, or curing illnesses.

St. Paul is a good example of a person with great faith, but whose request for a cure was denied. In his Second Letter to the Corinthians Paul confessed, "To keep me from being too elated, a thorn was given to me in the flesh, a messenger of Satan to torment me…. Three times I appealed to the Lord about this, that it would leave me, but he said to me, 'My strength is sufficient for you, for power is made perfect in weakness'" (see 12:7–9).

We are never told precisely what Paul's thorn was, but we are told that God chose not to take it away. In some mysterious fashion the suffering Paul had to endure had a good effect. He put it in mystical terms, "Whenever I am weak, then I am strong" (see 2 Corinthians 12:10).

The sacrament of the anointing, then, might be considered "the strength" which God gives to enable us to endure the negative for the sake of a positive. James, too, recognized this Christian mystery of enduring suffering: "My brothers and sisters, whenever you face trials of any kind, consider it nothing but joy, because you know that the testing of your faith produces endurance; and let endurance have its full effect, so that you may be mature and complete, lacking in nothing" (James 1:2–4).

Thy Will Be Done

You have probably heard the story of the man whose house was being flooded by a nearby river, and when a neighbor came to his rescue in a row boat, the homeowner refused the help, saying, "No, thank you! God will take care of me!" As the river continued to rise, the river patrol boat came by to provide rescue, but once again the man refused, assuring his would-be rescuers, "No! God will take care of me!" When the rising waters forced the man to the rooftop, a helicopter hovered overhead and through a bullhorn rescuers ordered the man to climb into the basket they had lowered. For the third time the man refused, shouting up to them, "No, God will take care of me!"

Later that day the floodwaters swept up over the roof and carried the man away to his death. When at last he came face-to-face with God, he expressed his disappointment: "God, I put my trust in you! I relied on you! I believed that you would take care of me! Why did you fail me?"

God said, "I did not let you down. I sent you a rowboat, a patrol boat, and a helicopter! My son, you have to accept the help I offer you in order to be saved!"

The best reason for receiving the sacrament of the anointing may simply be that through it God offers his help—whether it is God's healing or God's strength, which enables us to cope with illness or impending death.

As in all our prayers, the attitude we are to bring to the anointing of the sick is "Your will be done!" If God wants to cure us, we say, "Yes!" If God wants us to live with the illness, we say, "Yes!" If God want us to die, we say, "Yes!" This is the kind of faith that refuses to impose our will on God's plan. It is the kind of faith that characterized Mary's *fiat* to the Angel Gabriel's announcement that she was to be the Mother of Christ. It is the kind of trust that prompted Jesus's submission in the Garden of Gethsemane, "Not as I will it, but as you will it!"

The appropriate frame of mind and heart for receiving the sacrament of anointing is submission to God's will. It is as Jesus taught us to pray, "Thy will be done!" It is this openness to God's will that brings consolation and comfort and even joy. Priests who have anointed the terminally ill know from that experience that quite frequently the anointing brings to the patient visible signs of relief and peace.

Healing Body, Soul, and Spirit

Fr. Richstatter offers some insights into the effects of the sacrament and gives reasons why the sick should be anointed. He explains that physical healing is just one element of the grace available to us. He explains this view in more detail below.

* * *

When I first learned about extreme unction and about how sick one would have to be in order to be anointed, I thought of "sickness" exclusively in terms of bodily illness. I never thought that there might be serious illnesses whose principal causes or manifestations were not physical. Nor did I realize as I do now the holistic unity of body, soul, and spirit.

I should have known. For years I suffered from a colon disorder that my doctors said was caused by my unreasonable desire to make straight A's in every possible subject in school. That experience alone should have made me aware of the intimate relation of mind and body, but I never thought of "perfectionism" as a disease. Nor did I think of alcoholism as a disease; and I never even heard of codependency (a description of unhealthy relationships in a family affected by addiction). I was unaware how the actions of one member of a family can cause serious physical, mental, and spiritual illness in other members of the family.

Today one does not have to be a doctor to know that physical health is related to mental and spiritual health. We all know how a divorce can cause ulcers; how being overworked and run-down can make one more susceptible to the flu. Often a person who decides to withdraw from an addiction experiences not only physical pain but also suffers from anxiety and depression. Mothers have told me of how, after the physical trauma of childbirth, the joy of having a baby can be completely covered over by the hormonally induced postpartum depression that sometimes follows.

Today we are all aware that tensions, fear, and anxiety about the future affect not only our minds but our bodies as well. These illnesses can be serious. They can move us to ask for the healing touch of Christ in the sacrament of the anointing.

Persons with the disease of alcoholism or persons suffering from other addictions can be anointed. So can those who suffer from mental disorders. The anxiety before exploratory surgery to determine if cancer is present is a situation in which Christ's power can be invoked in the sacrament. Often the spouse or the principal caregiver of the person who is seriously ill also asks to be anointed when he or she, too, is seriously affected by the illness—the debilitating fear of an elderly husband ("How will I be able to live if she dies?"); the anguish of young parents whose child is dying ("How can a just and loving God allow this to happen?").

Our pastoral experience of the revised rite and the Church's desire for wider availability of the sacrament have helped pastors realize that serious mental and spiritual illnesses are also opportunities to celebrate this sacrament.

In these cases the person does not have to wait until the illness is so grave that he or she is in the hospital or institutionalized to celebrate the sacrament. Sacraments, after all, are community celebrations. It is preferable to celebrate them in the context of family and parish even before going to the hospital. The sick person has a better opportunity to appreciate the prayers and symbols of the rite when in her or his customary worshiping community.

There are times when old age and the fears and isolation that can sometimes accompany it need to be brought to the healing and comforting touch of Christ in this sacrament. It is a powerful sign for a parish community to see their senior members place their limitations and dependence in the hands of Christ, who accepted human limitation and freely embraced suffering and even death itself.

The anointing of the sick is a different kind of healing from a chemical placed into our bodies as a medicine or a surgical intervention to cut out diseased tissue. Sacraments are acts of faith; they grace the whole person—body, soul, and spirit. The blessing over the oil for anointing asks God to "send the power of your Holy Spirit, the Consoler, into this precious oil.... Make this oil a remedy for all who are anointed with it; heal them in body, in soul and in spirit, and deliver them from every affliction" (*Pastoral Care of the Sick*, 123).

The Purpose of Anointing Is to Make People Holy

Does it work? Will I experience healing? These are the questions that I am most frequently asked regarding the sacrament of anointing. And I always answer by saying yes. In my experience as a priest, healing always takes place. That healing, of course, is not restricted to mere physical healing.

When our attention is directed toward physical illness, it is natural to think of the effects of the sacrament in terms of physical healing. Sacraments, however, are celebrations of faith, expressions of who we are before God. This understanding of sacrament, together with the realization that we are more than our physical body, has led us to look again at the effects of the sacrament of anointing.

The Second Vatican Council has reminded us: "The purpose of the sacrament is to make people holy, to build up the Body of Christ and finally to give worship to God" (*Constitution on the Liturgy*, 59). The sacrament of the anointing of the sick accomplishes this by helping us gain insight into the religious meaning of human suffering.

A quote from the General Introduction to the ritual itself, in the *Pastoral Care of the Sick*, explains more: "Suffering and illness have always been among the greatest problems that trouble the human spirit. Christians feel and experience pain as do all other people; yet their faith helps them to grasp more deeply the mystery of suffering and to bear their pain with greater courage. From Christ's words they know that sickness has meaning and value for their own salvation and the salvation of the world. They also know that Christ, who during his life often visited and healed the sick, loves them in their illness" (1).

The celebration of the sacrament does not explain human suffering; sacraments are more than mere words of explanation. The sacraments celebrate faith. In the very celebrating we experience more and more who we are and what we believe. As the *Catechism of the Catholic Church* says, "Christ invites his disciples to follow him by taking up their cross in their turn. By following him they acquire a new outlook on illness and the sick" (*CCC*, 1506).

What does this new outlook involve? It helps us understand what St. Paul meant when he said: "Now I rejoice in my sufferings for your sake, and in my flesh I am filling up what is lacking in the afflictions of Christ on behalf of his body, which is the church" (Colossians 1:24).

It also sheds light on what St. Paul says in 2 Corinthians: "Power is made perfect in weakness. I will rather boast most gladly of my weaknesses, in order that the power of Christ may dwell with me" (see 2 Corinthians 12:9). In the sacrament, the sick come to see that "Jesus associates them with his own life of poverty and service. He makes them share in his ministry of compassion and healing" (*CCC*, 1506).

In the sacrament we pray that the sick be healed in body, in soul, and in spirit. God alone knows what kind of healing the sick need most: that a wound be healed, that a fear turn to confidence, that loneliness be embraced by the support of a praying community, that confusion in the face of all the whys—why me? why suffering? why now?—turn to insight.

The sacrament of the anointing of the sick does not remove the mystery of human suffering. Yet its celebration gives us a window into the mystery of a loving God. Our loving God raises up the crucified Son to display his victorious wounds, sitting triumphant at the Father's right hand.

How Do We Receive the Sacrament of Anointing?
The Basics

Current Church practice requires a priest to be the minister of the sacrament. The so-called "matter" of the sacrament is olive oil (though in some circumstances oil derived from other plants is permitted). The oil must be blessed by a bishop (though in some circumstances a priest may bless the oil). Usually the oil is blessed by the bishop during Holy Week and then is distributed to parishes and reserved in a case especially for the *olea sancta* ("holy oils").

The ritual for the sacrament of the anointing lists three distinct parts in the celebration of the sacrament: (1) the prayer of faith; (2) the laying on of hands; and (3) the anointing with oil.

The prayer of faith is the community asking for God's help for the sick person. The whole Church is represented by the priest and any others who surround the sick person. The prayers for the sick include the following prayer, which is prayed during the act of anointing: "Through this holy anointing may the Lord in his love and mercy help you with the grace of the Holy Spirit. May the Lord who frees you from sin save you and raise you up."

The laying on of hands is that part of the ritual which recalls and repeats the action of Jesus who frequently laid hands on the sick as a sign of blessing. We remember the description in Luke's Gospel: "As the sun was setting, all those who had any who were sick with various kinds of diseases brought them to him; and he laid his hands on each of them and cured them" (4:40).

The anointing with oil is on the forehead and on the hands of the sick person (though in some circumstances a single anointing on the head or another part of the body is permitted). The anointing is accompanied by the priest's prayer.

Who Is Anointed?

The seriously ill or those facing serious medical procedures are candidates for the sacrament of the sick. The elderly too may be anointed if there is noticeable weakness or decline in health, even if no serious illness is diagnosed. Seriously ill children may receive the anointing if they would be helped by receiving the sacrament.

The sacrament should not be delayed until a person is dying. The revision mandated by the Second Vatican Council confirmed that "as soon as anyone of the faithful begins to be in danger of death from sickness or old age, the fitting time for him or her to receive the sacrament has certainly already arrived." The Council recognized that the sacrament is more fittingly called "anointing of the sick" rather than "extreme unction."

Among many older Catholics the old notion still lingers that the anointing is only for those near death or that calling for the priest implies the sick person is dying. Most priests are eager to change the "emergency mentality" which calls for them to come for an anointing at the last minute.

A sick person may be anointed a second time if the illness worsens, or if a second disease is diagnosed. An unconscious person may be anointed if it can reasonably be supposed that he or she would want to receive the sacrament. A dead person is not to be anointed, though the priest may judge that a person at the point of death (if not already anointed) may receive the anointing.

The Rites in Various Settings

The sacrament of the anointing of the sick may be administered during Mass. Many parishes have an anointing within Mass to accommodate, at one time and with the community, the anointing of several parishioners who are ill or elderly. The Mass opens with a welcoming statement, reminding those present about Christ's concern for the sick and his healing power. After the Liturgy of the Word, the priest-presider begins the Liturgy of Anointing, which usually includes a litany, a prayer over the oil, the laying on of hands, and the anointing. If there is a large number to be anointed, other priests may assist. Mass then continues as usual.

Parishes may also schedule an anointing outside Mass, which includes welcoming rites, reading from Scripture, the Liturgy of the Anointing, and, in some circumstances, a Liturgy of Holy Communion.

Probably the most frequently used rite is the one for anointing in a hospital or institution. It is an abbreviated ritual, which consists of a greeting, recollection of James's words about calling the elders to anoint the sick, and then the anointing liturgy, including the Lord's Prayer. This simplified rite is intended for use in emergency situations or when only the priest and the sick person are present. The full rite is preferred where possible.

The Celebration of Viaticum

Intimately connected to the sacrament of the anointing of the sick, though different from it, is the practice of bringing Holy Communion to a person who is in danger of death or actively dying. The Eucharist in this setting is called Viaticum, from the Latin word for "journeying." In secular use *viaticum* was "money for the journey." A farewell meal was called *viatica cena*. The Church appropriated the term to describe Holy Communion for those near death.

Church law stipulates that the Christian faithful in danger of death are to be nourished by Holy Communion (canon 921.1). This practice is so important in the mind of the Church that the law prescribes that even if the sick person already received Communion on a given day, if the sick person's condition worsens, Holy Communion may be offered again on the same day. In fact the law notes that as long as the danger of death lasts, it is recommended that Holy Communion be given to the sick person, but on separate days (canons 921.2–3).

When Holy Communion is given as Viaticum, the ceremony has additional prayers. If circumstances allow, the Liturgy for Viaticum includes a penitential rite, a Scripture reading, a homily, a renewal of baptismal promises, a brief litany, the Lord's Prayer, and the distribution of Communion. The prayers may even include the so-called "Apostolic Pardon," the use of a special authority from the pope to grant a person full pardon and remission of all sins.

Ideally the celebration of Viaticum takes place during Mass, but in many, if not most, circumstances the sick person is confined to a hospital or nursing home or is in an emergency situation thereby making Mass impracticable. Those who cannot receive Holy Communion under the form of bread may receive under the form of wine if the Blood of the Lord is available on this occasion.

Pastoral Care of the Sick

Conscious of Jesus's example and mindful of the call to compassion, the Church strongly urges that special attention and care be shown to the sick and dying. In addition to the sacrament of the anointing of the sick, the Church brings together in the *Pastoral Care of the Sick* encouragement, directions, and rituals for responding to those who are ill or dying.

Clergy and laity alike are reminded to visit the sick, to help them pray, to share with them God's Word, to show the community's love and compassion. Jesus considered our visits to the sick as one of the occasions in which we serve him. "I was sick and you took care of me…when was it that we saw you sick?… I tell you, just as you did it to one of the least of these who are members of my family, you did it to me" (see Matthew 25:36–40).

Commendation of the Dying

Although it is not a sacrament in itself, one of the consolations the Church offers to the dying and to their family and friends is the ritual of prayer commending the dying patient to the care of the saints and the Lord. The rite is to be adapted to the circumstances, but it includes reading aloud short texts from Scripture (e.g., "Who can separate us from the love of Christ?"), longer readings from the Bible, the litany of the saints, and, when the moment of death seems near, prayers of commendation, such as "Go forth, Christian soul, from this world.... May you live in peace this day."

And once death has occurred, there are prayers calling on the saints and angels to come forth to meet the departed and lead the deceased into eternal light. In addition there are prayers for the survivors, asking God to show compassion to the grieving.

Prayers for the Dead

The priest, deacon, or layperson may also lead family and friends in prayers for the dead: "In this moment of sorrow the Lord is in our midst.... Almighty God, hear our prayers for your son/daughter whom you have called from this life to yourself...hear our prayers and be merciful...."

Moments of Grace

Later still, the Church embraces the survivors as well as the deceased in its funeral liturgy and burial rites. This outreach stems from the Church's conviction that God made each person for eternal life. Jesus, by his death and resurrection, broke the chains of sin and death, which had been holding humanity back. The Church, in its funeral rites, offers praise and thanks to God for the life now retuned to its creator. In the process of praying for the dead and commending them to God, the Church is able to offer sympathy and comfort to those who grieve.

In times of sorrow and loss we are out of control and most vulnerable, aware of our mortality and often questioning the meaning of life. Sickness, dying, and funerals are moments of grace when we seek help, when we are open to God's plan, when we grow in our spiritual lives.

Questions for Reflection

1. How can the sacrament of anointing heal those who are sick or dying? What other physical, emotional, or spiritual effects might the sacrament have?
2. What is the value of having communal anointing of the sick?
3. Can we ask for healing and still be honest when we say, "Thy will be done"?

Conclusion

The sacrament of reconciliation and the sacrament of the anointing of the sick are Jesus's response to the brokenness, vulnerability, and mortality of the human race. In our more honest moments we realize that we are not perfect, that we are not in control of our lives. This humble acknowledgment does not demoralize us or lead us to depression. Rather the awareness that we are weak leads us to ask for forgiveness, to be forgiving, to seek God's help in our daily lives.

Neither of these sacraments is magic, nor are they superstitions. Instead they are points of contact between Jesus and us. They are part of the legacy of his mission: "I came that they may have life, and have it abundantly" (see John 10:10). The Church inherited Jesus's concern and through the sacraments continues what he did. In reconciliation and in anointing we experience Jesus's healing touch. How comforting to know that Jesus is still healing, still forgiving, still very much with us.

St. Catherine of Siena once remarked, "All the way to heaven is heaven, because Jesus said, 'I am the way.'" The sacraments are occasions when Jesus's presence becomes quite palpable, even intense. He's there all along the journey. And in the moments when we feel worthless and out-of-sorts, his sacraments of healing bring comfort and the assurance that it is heaven all the way!

Sources

DeGidio, Sandra, O.S.M., "The Sacrament of Reconciliation: Celebrating God's Forgiveness," *Catholic Update,* March 1986.

———. "The Seven Sacraments: Symbols of God's Care," *Catholic Update*, April 1983.

Foley, Leonard, O.F.M., "Why Confess My Sins? The Bishops' Synod Asks Us to Take Another Look," *Catholic Update*, March 1984.

Richstatter, Thomas, O.F.M., "Anointing the Sick: A Parish Sacrament," *Catholic Update*, January 1996.

———. "How to Celebrate the Sacrament of Reconciliation Today," *Catholic Update*, August 2000.

———. "Sacrament of Reconciliation: Celebrating the Mercy of God," *Catholic Update,* June 2009.

———. *The Sacraments: How Catholics Pray* (Cincinnati: St. Anthony Messenger Press, 1995).

Contributors

Sandra DeGidio, O.S.M., is a freelance writer, lecturer, and spiritual guide. She is the author of *RCIA: The Rites Revisited* (Harper and Row), and *Reconciliation: Sacrament With a Future* (St. Anthony Messenger Press).

Leonard Foley, O.F.M., priest, popular religious educator, and retreat director, is the author of *Believing In Jesus* and many other books from Franciscan Media.

Thomas Richstatter, O.F.M., a priest with a doctorate in liturgy and sacramental theology, is a popular writer and lecturer at St. Meinrad (Indiana) School of Theology.